The Guide to Low-Cost Divorce in Virginia

Virginia L. Colin, Ph.D.
and
Rebecca A. Martin, CPA

Also by Virginia L. Colin
Human Attachment

Also by Rebecca A. Martin
How to Get Divorced For Free in California

Early Reviews of

The Guide to Low-Cost Divorce in Virginia

This Guide is forthright, practical and clearly presented in readable English. I appreciate the fact that the authors are able to demystify the process while recognizing the comprehensive impact of divorce -- the emotional impact on spouses as well as children, the financial fallout, and even the challenge of dividing household assets. The questions that are posed throughout the book help the reader organize data, identify priorities, and become educated about the practical details of a legal process. Whether paying a professional mediator to craft your parenting plan and separation agreement, or resorting to the services of attorneys to hammer out the details, this Guide to Low-Cost Divorce is a must read. Each party is then educated about the homework that is required to proceed with efficiency, less stress and better solutions. – Dorothy D. Taft

A very quick read, clear, and informative book. I will be recommending it to my clients. – Experienced Family Mediator

Contents

CHAPTER 4

Helping Your Kids Manage This Difficult
Transition

CHAPTER 5

CHAPTER 6

CHAPTER 7

Introduction

Divorce can be tough, scary, and expensive. You have to deal with emotional issues, financial issues, and legal issues. If you have children, you also have to address their needs. Our goal is to simplify the process for you. We will show you how to avoid unnecessary turmoil and distress and how to save lots of time and money as you manage these issues. Then you can move on with confidence. If you are currently feeling overwhelmed, spinning your wheels, and wasting your time, this book can help you.

About saving money: Even for people with little wealth, a litigated divorce can easily cost $20,000 to $100,000 in attorney fees. We will tell you how you may be able to negotiate and arrange your divorce without paying more than $1,500 to $3,000 to lawyers and/or a mediator.

About saving time: The period of time from the date of filing for divorce to the date of completing a litigated divorce is usually fourteen months to two and a half years. Before you can file for divorce on most grounds in Virginia, you must wait until you have been separated for many months: at least six if you have no minor children, at least twelve if you have a minor child. When you add the period of separation to the time that passes after you file for divorce, you and your children may be living an unsettled, distressed life for two or three years. As an alternative, we will show you how to negotiate and commit to the terms of your divorce much sooner. Your life can be settled and your plans made and implemented as soon as you and your spouse are ready, which may be long before you can file for divorce. From the date of filing to the date of completing an uncontested divorce can be as little as two weeks in some jurisdictions.

This book grew from Rebecca Martin's earlier book about handling her separation and divorce in California, getting her kids settled, and moving on with her life. Throughout this journey she was determined to get a great result for herself and her kids at the lowest cost possible. With help from an attorney friend and with information from others who had been through the process, she found numerous free resources. You can do the same. In the end, all Rebecca paid for her uncontested divorce was the court filing fee.

The laws and court procedures in the Commonwealth of Virginia are very different from the laws and procedures in the state of California. Much of what Rebecca wrote about the emotional and financial aspects of divorce applies almost anywhere in the USA. Co-author Virginia Colin has added some thoughts to those sections and has added information about the laws and procedures in Virginia.

It is important for you to know from the beginning that neither author is an attorney or a therapist. Rebecca handled her own divorce in California and Virginia handled her own divorce in Maryland, so we can teach you a lot based on our own experiences. In addition,

Virginia Colin is trained, certified, and experienced as a family mediator in the Commonwealth of Virginia and therefore can give you a good amount of *information* about relevant statutes. What we cannot do is give you *legal advice* about what you should do, given the specifics of your situation. We strongly recommend that you consult a family law attorney early in the process. On July first each year minor or major changes to laws about divorce and related matters may occur. Consequently you need to get up-to-date advice.

This book is not intended to be all-inclusive. It is partly Rebecca's story of how she navigated the emotional, financial, and legal aspects of divorce. It is partly a guide to help you do the same, but in a different state and with some additional information and advice. If you want a roadmap to help you handle your divorce mostly as a do-it-yourself process, thereby saving huge amounts of money, then we wrote this guide for you.

Specifically, we will give you good ideas about:

- how to set the stage for an inexpensive divorce, gather information, and avoid some pitfalls

- where to find good Internet resources. You do not need to buy expensive legal guides about do-it-yourself divorces, filled with all kinds of legal forms, software, and details.

- how to get some free or nearly free legal advice about your specific legal questions

- how to take good care of yourself as your life changes in big ways

- how you can make the family changes easier for your kids to handle

- how to get free or low-cost, good-quality therapy for your kids if they need additional help

- how to structure a solid co-parenting plan

- how to work with a reluctant or argumentative spouse, because getting an inexpensive divorce does depend partly on your spouse's willingness to participate and cooperate

Avoiding legal jargon, we will explain the steps in a way that is easy to follow. This guide will help you move down the path toward a constructive divorce and, we hope, help you feel relieved and empowered.

CHAPTER 1

Laying the Groundwork for an Inexpensive, Constructive Divorce

When divorcing, a good goal is to work things out in an amicable fashion so that both parties can move on. It is especially important to stay civil and cooperative if you have children who are under 18 years old or still in high school.

This book is primarily for people who have already decided to divorce. Maybe you feel sure that divorce is the right step to take. Maybe your spouse has made it clear that he or she insists on getting divorced. Maybe the marriage was damaging to one or both of you. Maybe you are just too different to make a marriage work, and the best solution is to let it go. Maybe your marriage was a great success for a good number of years, but your lives have gone in different directions and you no longer feel that you belong together.

If you have kids and keeping the family together in a healthy way seems like a real possibility, that goal is worth pursuing. If you are not sure about proceeding toward a divorce – if there is still some hope for a healthy reconciliation – you may want to work with a marriage counselor or with a family mediator who has experience helping people negotiate healing separation agreements. That work can help you reach clarity about continuing or ending your marriage. If you then decide to divorce, you can come back to this guide. This book is not about how to save your marriage; it is about what to do when you have decided to divorce.

After getting past her initial shock and anger, Rebecca realized that she wanted to resolve her divorce as quickly, as painlessly, and as inexpensively as possible. She did not want to have to battle it out in court. Because the divorce process was new for her, she did not know what would happen. You may be in the same situation.

Once you have decided to get a divorce, where do you begin? For Rebecca, taking action brought a feeling of being more in control and empowered. She was not passively waiting for her husband to get the process started. Luckily for her, she and her husband initially agreed about a number of issues. Consequently she wanted to get moving quickly, in case he changed his mind or decided to make things more difficult later.

Even if your spouse seems cooperative and agreeable, it is still advisable to proceed with caution. We will have more to say about that later.

No matter how quickly or slowly you want to move, you need to get your financial records in order. Some couples separate and know they want to divorce but, because they think the process will be difficult and expensive, they do not take action for years. For most people, delaying makes it much more difficult to retrieve and compile financial statements and other necessary details. Most people dislike the unsettling feeling of having unfinished business hanging over their heads. For others, however, waiting provides time they need so that they can calm down and handle their divorce in a sensible, low-cost way.

The process of divorcing does not have to be difficult or expensive, especially when you have this guide to help you. When you and your spouse have made your decisions and put them into a written, signed agreement, you can handle the necessary court paperwork on your own.

The personal issues and emotions can be difficult. Coming to agreement with your spouse can be difficult. You may want some advice from an attorney, some assistance from a family mediator, and some support from a counselor as your negotiate the terms of your divorce. On their own or with that modest amount of support, most people can work out parenting plans and property settlement terms and proceed to an uncontested divorce.

Getting started and taking action can help you feel more in control. In addition, both you and anyone you date in the future are likely to be glad when this process has been completed. Finalizing your divorce will no longer be on your chore list. It will be clear that you are free to move on independently, have fun dating if you want to, and maybe find a new love.

Some Simple Steps to Get Started

1. Get organized. Get some file folders for storing all divorce-related paperwork. Label them and use them.

2. Gather account statements for assets and debts that are in your name, in your spouse's name, and jointly owned.

3. Start keeping track of details. For example, if your spouse orally agrees to give you the dining room furniture, write it down, date it, and have your spouse sign it.

4. Begin keeping a record of when your kids are with you and when they are with your spouse.

Financial Records You May Need

We hope that you have kept good financial records throughout your marriage. To make well-informed decisions, you will need them. If you have not kept good records, start gathering the documents you need. You may need documents that verify the value and ownership (just one spouse, or shared ownership) of your assets. You may need to know their value when you bought them, when you married, and when you separated. Similarly, you may need documents that verify the amounts and ownership of your debts.

People with few assets and few debts often make their financial decisions on their own. People with more wealth and more complex financial situations sometimes ask professionals to help them understand their finances.

Assets may include:

- Real estate

- Timeshares

- Cars, boats, and other vehicles

- Bank accounts

- Brokerage accounts

- Pensions

- Retirement accounts

- Jewelry

- Furniture

- Computers and phones

- Household items

Liabilities may include:

- Mortgages

- Vehicle loans

- Credit card accounts

- Student loans

- Unsecured loans

- Loans from your 401K, IRA, or other retirement accounts

The lists above are sufficient for many people but do not include all possible types of assets and debts. If you already have an accountant or a financial advisor, you may want to ask him or her to help you make sure that your lists of assets and debts are complete. If you like working with spreadsheets, you can use the asset list above to start one spreadsheet that lists your assets, their values, and, for real estate and vehicles, whose name is on the deed or title. You can use the liabilities list to make a second spreadsheet that lists your debts and whose name is associated with each debt.

You will need to figure out which assets are marital property and which are separate property, owned by just one of you. Similarly, you will need to figure out or jointly decide which debts belong to the two of you as marital debts, which debts are entirely your responsibility to pay, and which are entirely your spouse's responsibility.

If you have children, you may want to postpone some decisions about assets and debts until you have made some preliminary decisions about parenting arrangements and short-term financial support for the unemployed or low-wage spouse and the children. For the sake of coherence, we are nevertheless including quite a bit of information about property distribution here. If you need to attend to other matters first, you can return to this section later.

In Virginia, almost all property either of you acquired during your marriage is presumed to be jointly owned. In particular, income earned by either spouse during the marriage is marital property. That includes income that has been stored in retirement accounts and income that was earned during your marriage but has not yet been paid, such as a year-end bonus. Gifts from one spouse to the other may also be treated as marital property in Virginia. You are expected to divide marital property and other assets equitably after you pay any debts secured by them. "Equitable" means fair, considering all relevant factors, but not necessarily equal.

As a general rule, property you owned prior to the marriage, property you inherited, and property you received as a gift to you as an individual from someone other than your spouse is your separate property. You are not required by law to share it with your spouse. Income received from separate property, such as rental income from a house you inherited, is also separate property. Exceptions occur when you have complicated the picture by mixing separate property with marital property.

Separate property that does not have to be shared with your spouse also ordinarily includes income you earned after you separated.

If you and your spouse have commingled separate property with joint property, it can be hard to figure out how much of the value of the mixed asset should still go to its original owner. For example, if one spouse contributed $100,000 from separate property to buy a house that both spouses bought together and lived in for ten years, and the value of the equity in the house is now $300,000, how much of that value should belong to each spouse? What if the spouse who did not have $100,000 to contribute to the purchase price did most of the work to add a sunroom to the house, thereby increasing its value?

Most people reading this book will be able to figure out or decide on a fair way to divide their assets and debts. If you have a complicated asset, such as the value of a business that one spouse built up while the other spouse was a stay-at-home parent, you should talk with an attorney. Similarly, if you have commingled separate property and marital property and are having trouble agreeing on a fair way to divide the resulting assets, you may want to seek legal advice. Even in complicated situations, however, Virginia has seen many couples develop plans for dividing assets and debts that both parties thought were equitable and acceptable.

Some people want input from lawyers and financial analysts before making these decisions. Many people are comfortable deciding how to divide assets and debts on their own or with help from a mediator.

Records to Keep and Things to Be Careful about if You Have Kids Together

If you have kids, it is a good idea to start keeping track of the details of your life in a written record. If you ever do need to go to court to ask for a ruling about when your kids will be with each of their parents, you will be glad that you have such records. Rebecca used a pocket calendar to keep track of when her kids were in her care and when they were in her husband's care. You may find an app that makes recording such details easy for you, or you can simply use good old-fashioned pen and paper.

Starting now, keep good records of important conversations, whether they occur in email, in text messages, or through other communication channels. If you ever do end up in court, you will have records that may provide good evidence for your case. Keep detailed records of everything, including anything that could show bad behavior on your spouse's part. Do not, however, record the other person in a private conversation without his or her permission. Doing so may be illegal, and the recording would probably not be admissible in court.

Rebecca kept every bit of email correspondence between her and her husband that said anything about the kids, about dividing assets and debts, or about her character and competence. A word of caution: Be mindful that an email is a written record that could one day be used against you. If you are feeling outraged, be careful what you say in email. No matter how amicable you think your divorce will be, until it is final you cannot know what will happen. You would not want to find yourself in court defending your character after your spouse presented a string of vitriolic email messages you wrote while you were overly emotional.

In addition, be careful on social networking sites. What you say can come back to bite you. Rebecca knows of a woman who lost primary custody of her child in part due to comments she had made on a friend's Facebook wall. Don't let this happen to you. You do not have to be an angel, but you do need to avoid looking crazy, acting irresponsibly, and committing libel (making false statements that damage someone's reputation). Assume that anything you post on Facebook or on any other social networking site will eventually be available to everyone in the world, because a friend of a friend of a friend may see it and forward it to your worst enemy.

Even after you are divorced, be careful in email and on social media. Until your kids are 18 years old and through high school, custody, visitation, and child support can change if circumstances change. For example, if one of you loses your job, gets a big raise, moves, remarries, or experiences other major changes in your lives, then changes in child support and/or changes in your shared parenting plan (otherwise known as custody and visitation) may be appropriate. Do not put anything private or confidential in such a public venue. In addition, your kids may one day see things that you have posted on social media. These rather public forums are not good places to vent your frustrations about your ex.

In addition to keeping records about what your ex is doing (or not doing when he or she should be doing it), be careful not to sabotage yourself. For example, if you want significant time with your children, don't move far away from your spouse without evaluating the consequences. Think big decisions through and discuss them with friends, relatives, and/or a counselor who is experienced in family and parenting issues. When the right time comes, also discuss big decisions with your ex.

Also be careful about any situation in which you may be viewed as using poor judgment or behaving badly. Examples include excessive partying, DUIs, documented angry outbursts, or anything that could give your spouse evidence to depict you negatively. Any irresponsible behavior could serve as ammunition to limit your time with your children.

In the best case divorce scenario, you and your spouse will both be reasonable and will agree about what plans are good for your kids and what settlement terms are fair. The above is just a warning to be careful, especially if either you or your spouse feels angry or vengeful. Occasionally a spouse who seemed cooperative becomes hostile and drags the process into an unexpected court battle. Keep your behavior respectable, especially if you hope that your children's primary home will be with you.

Living Separately Under One Roof

The Commonwealth of Virginia requires spouses to live "separate and apart" for a period of months before they can file for a no-fault divorce: twelve months if you have a minor child; six months if you do not have minor children and do have a written, signed agreement that settles all issues. If you and your spouse are on a tight budget but want to divorce, you may need to plan carefully and wait a while before one of you moves out. In the meantime, the law allows you to live separately under one roof. If you meet the requirements of the law, the weeks or months during which you live separately under one roof do count as part of the period that is required before you can file for divorce. Continuing to live in the same house may be quite stressful, given that you intend to divorce, but it may be your best option from a financial perspective.

To make this arrangement work, you must truly live as if each of you were already single (except that, unlike a single person, you probably cannot have sex with anyone without risking legal consequences when you divorce). Sleeping in separate bedrooms is not enough. You must live separate lives. Do not buy groceries for each other, cook for each other, eat meals together, do each other's laundry, or socialize as a couple. To get a thorough understanding of what counts as living separately at the same address, you can do some Internet research and may want to talk with an attorney. You will need a witness to verify that you lived separate lives even though you were under one roof. Some judges require more evidence than others to convince them that you were not cohabiting while you were living at the same address. Your witness may have to be someone who has visited often, knows one of you well, and has fairly detailed knowledge about how you lived during your period of separation.

Just as if you were in separate apartments, however, you and your spouse can decide all the terms of your divorce, put them into an enforceable Agreement, and even separate all or almost all of your assets and debts long before you file for divorce. If both of you are ready, it is in your power to take action and move on with your lives.

CHAPTER 2

Keeping Costs Down

Lawyers Are Expensive

The approach Virginia (the author) recommends for most people is as follows: Early in the process, do some research on the Internet and maybe in books. Then ask a mediation-friendly lawyer for advice about your rights, your responsibilities, and what is reasonable to expect. Next, negotiate directly with your spouse to resolve everything that is easy to resolve. Then work with a family mediator to resolve the matters that are hard to resolve and to prepare a draft Agreement. When you and your spouse have a draft Agreement, ask an attorney to look it over to make sure that your interests are adequately protected. This way you pay for very little of a lawyer's time, but you get the legal advice you need. For most people, there is no need to pay thousands of dollars to retain an attorney to represent you and speak for you. You can pay just for the time and advice you actually need. You may even be able to get legal advice for free. We will say more about that later.

We definitely want to honor the attorneys who put their clients' needs ahead of their own financial gain. Virginia knows many family law attorneys who are sincere about trying to help their clients reach reasonable settlements reasonably quickly. Having two attorneys talk to each other on your behalf is still more expensive than talking directly with each other, but we do not want to give good lawyers bad reputations. There are some very good people earning their livings as family law attorneys and doing it with compassion and integrity.

Unfortunately, other attorneys are less admirable. They have a financial incentive to keep your case unresolved for as long as possible, and some lawyers respond to that incentive. Rebecca has an attorney friend whose bosses at more than one family law firm reprimanded him when he settled cases. He was told to instigate conflict so that the firm would collect more money. The more contentious and difficult your case becomes, the more money the lawyers get. For some lawyers, the goal is to add fuel to the fires, not to help you reach a reasonable settlement. Seek recommendations, do some research about various lawyers' approaches, and avoid exploitive, contentious attorneys. They are the opposite of helpful.

Rebecca knows another attorney who works exclusively with high net worth clients. That lawyer frequently sees clients who pay attorney fees that add up to more than the value of the assets the parties are fighting about. She has had clients who paid their lawyers two million dollars while fighting over assets worth only one and a half million dollars. What a waste! That sort of experience is extremely destructive to the couple and to their children, leaving not only financial damage but also emotional scars that last for years or even decades. Do not give a huge amount of your money to lawyers unless you really have no better way to resolve matters.

When deciding whether to hire an attorney or not, do a cost-benefit analysis. You can ask attorneys how much they charge for each hour of their time and how many hours they think they will need to accomplish a certain task. If you have to spend $15,000 to hire an attorney to gather evidence and represent you at a spousal support hearing, is it worth it? For example, if you think hiring the attorney will reduce the amount of spousal support that you have to pay by $300 per month, is it worth paying $15,000 on attorney fees? At $300 per month, it will take you $15,000 \div 300 = 50$ months (more than 4 years) to recoup that cost. And that is IF the attorney succeeds in obtaining the spousal support reduction for you. Often people do not get the results they wanted and expected even when they have paid large sums to lawyers. Family law attorneys do not work on a contingency basis. Even when they lose, you still have to pay them. Lawyers' fees vary from one part of the state to another, but $300 or more per hour is not at all unusual. At that rate, the bills can quickly add up to a large sum.

We suggest that you do the math and consider all the angles before hiring an attorney. If a lawyer can add enough value, then hire one. For example, if it seems likely that the lawyer can save you $25,000 on some disputed financial issue, paying him or her $10,000 to do so may be reasonable. Similarly, if a lawyer can help you get time with your kids that you would not have won without the lawyer's assistance, hiring the lawyer may be worth the price. Just be careful to find out how likely it is that the lawyer can truly help you. Some lawyers, eager to have your business, may tell you what you want to hear without providing any evidence that they can get a better outcome for you than you would get without their assistance.

As previously noted, an option well worth considering is hiring an attorney to advise you as needs arise without retaining an attorney to do everything for you. You can pay, by the hour, just for the advice you need. You can do your own negotiating, with help from a skilled family mediator if needed.

This book is about taking the least expensive good road possible. That means not involving attorneys more than you need to. It's your money. Spend it on what matters most to you.

Doing everything completely on your own without getting any legal advice is risky. If you sign an Agreement, it will affect your future rights and obligations. For that reason, when you have a draft Agreement that you developed on your own or with help from a mediator, it is a good idea to ask a mediation-friendly attorney to look it over before you sign it.

To Mediate or Not to Mediate

A mediator is an impartial professional whose job is to help you and your spouse negotiate constructively in a private, confidential setting and, if possible, develop an Agreement. Even if the mediator is an attorney, he or she is not allowed to give you legal advice. Your mediator can never act as either party's attorney. His or her only role is to help you and your spouse become well informed and create an agreement that you both believe is good for your children and includes acceptable terms about financial matters.

If you and your spouse can work everything out on your own, you may not need a mediator at all. If you cannot reach agreement about *all* of the important questions, working with a mediator can save you a lot of time, a lot of money, and a lot of anguish. Litigating issues is expensive, time-consuming, and distressing. Paying lawyers to negotiate on your behalf is more expensive than working with a mediator. One reason is that you and your spouse can pay one mediator to help you resolve your disagreements instead of paying two attorneys for each single hour of negotiation. If the mediator charges $250 per hour and the attorneys each charge $300 per hour, then you are paying $250 per hour instead of $600 per hour as you move toward a settlement. The savings are actually greater than that, because in addition to each attorney talking with the other attorney, your attorney has to spend time (and your money) talking with you to find out what you want and whether a settlement proposal is okay with you. The financial savings when you hire a mediator are huge – usually thousands of dollars.

Parenthetically, about half of the family mediators in some areas are attorneys. The ones who are attorneys sometimes charge about twice as much as the ones who are not attorneys. We have not seen evidence that the mediators who are attorneys help people develop

Agreements twice as fast as other mediators do. Some mediators who are also attorneys have truly learned the attentive, supportive, facilitative skills mediators need. Others attorneys who say they can mediate have not left their training as adversarial advocates behind. When choosing a mediator, do some research and, if possible, get recommendations from people you trust.

All mediators who are certified by the Supreme Court of Virginia to handle cases referred to them from Circuit Courts have had to learn a good amount of family law. This includes the certified family mediators who are not lawyers. You can find certified mediators in your area at http://www.courts.state.va.us/courtadmin/aoc/djs/progra ms/drs/mediation/searchable_mediator_directory.html.

If you and your spouse are able to agree about all relevant issues and develop a written Agreement on your own, that will be the cheapest route. Be careful, however. You may get what you pay for. For most people, checking with at least one professional – a certified, professional family mediator and/or a lawyer – would be wise. There may be things that you do not know you should include in your Agreement. For example, did you know that what your spouse earned between the date of marriage and the date of separation and put into his or her retirement is a marital asset? In other words, it belongs to both of you even though it is in an account that has only one person's name on it. Did you know that if you waive spousal support (alimony) in your Property Settlement Agreement and fail to reserve the right to request a modification of spousal support later, then you will probably *never* be able to get spousal support? Courts in Virginia cannot award spousal support in any way that differs from what you put into your signed Agreement.

If you and your spouse think you have agreed about everything, you may still want to discuss your decisions with a family mediator to increase your confidence that you are making well-informed decisions. Acting as your scrivener, a mediator can write your Parenting Plan (still called custody and visitation in Virginia), Spousal and Child Support Agreement, and Property Settlement Agreement for you. Many ex-couples include all of those matters in one comprehensive Agreement. You can have an attorney look each Agreement over before you sign it.

Methods for Developing an Agreement on Your Own

No matter how amicable your relationship with your soon-to-be-ex spouse is, and no matter how simple things may seem on the surface, divorce is seldom easy. For most people, blue skies are ahead, even if it is hard to see them now. Sometimes you need to take a leap of faith. Sometimes you need to get through current hard times and find out later what else is possible in your life.

Try your best to find some common ground on which you and your spouse can both win. For instance, if children are involved, focus on them and on what is going to be best for them. Don't spend your time and energy seeking emotional justice, retaliating for something that happened during the marriage, or focusing on anything else that you think is going to hurt or offend your spouse and so make negotiating difficult.

If you are struggling with coming to an agreement with your soon-to-be ex, take time to strategize and figure out what will appeal most to him or her and also accomplish what both of you want to do. Here are some strategies to consider.

1. Appeal to his or her pocketbook. Instead of spending $300 per person per hour for attorneys, develop a settlement agreement on your own and use the money saved for a better purpose. For example, if you believe that the total cost for a mediator and/or attorneys would be $21,000, but you educate yourself enough to be able to do almost all of the work yourselves, most of that $21,000 can be used toward a child's college fund.

2. Consider counseling or therapy: If you or your spouse can't get past the angry or hurt feelings, therapy (either individual or group therapy) may be the best path to help one or both of you, separately, make peace with the idea of divorce. Many people have trouble agreeing about parenting plans or financial questions because of residual hurt and/or angry feelings. If the negative emotions can be addressed through therapy, agreement is much more likely. If you have minor children and will therefore be co-parenting for years to come, it is especially important to resolve emotional issues as well as you can.

Therapists are less expensive and more effective than attorneys when you need to deal with blame, rage, helplessness, or other emotions. Many people waste huge amounts of time and money paying their attorneys to listen to them vent their angry complaints about their spouses. All that does is run up the bills from the attorneys. There is little or no benefit to the clients. Paying a therapist costs less and is better for your psychological and spiritual health.

As much as possible, take care of your therapy issues before going to your attorney or mediator. You may not even realize how much your conversations with your attorney are costing you until you get your bill. Resist the urge to call your attorney or mediator each time you get into an argument with your spouse or some other event causes an emotional reaction. Instead, allow some time for the acute emotions to pass, or, if you are very upset, call a therapist. You will have more money left in your bank account, and you will probably get better help.

3. Inventory all of your marital property. Make a list of all your shared vehicles, furniture, household goods, works of art, and other items. Then make a copy of the list and give it to your spouse. For each item on the list, mark whether you want it, don't want it, or are indifferent. Ask your spouse to do the same. Then compare your lists. Right away it will be easy to identify the items that you want that your spouse does not want, and vice versa. This way you'll start on a good note by agreeing on some things. You can postpone decisions about the more difficult items to a later time. This

strategy will allow you to make some decisions right away. Both of you will see that you are making progress.

When it comes to negotiating about your shared personal property, it is also important to estimate the value of the property you are dividing. You probably do not need to pay to have items appraised. The two of you can compare your furniture and other possessions with similar items on Craigslist or eBay to estimate what each item is worth. Unless you have truly unique possessions, someone is probably selling something similar online. Most used property, including yours, is not really worth much.

If one of you ends up with things that have a higher total value, the other can get an equalizing payment from the liquid assets (cash) so that the overall division of assets is fair.

4. Take the high road. This often yields the best results. You actually get more of what you want when you show that you are concerned with the best outcome for everyone involved, not just for yourself. If you sound selfish or manipulative, your spouse may be unwilling to develop an agreement with you. If you sincerely take the high road, you may inspire your spouse to do the same.

5. Focus on solutions. No matter how emotional you or your soon-to-be-ex may be at any given time, try to come back to the main goal of finding a solution that will work for both of you and will allow you to live apart

harmoniously. It is OK at times to listen to some of your spouse's concerns over issues that are essentially distractions, not important issues. This keeps the dialogue open. You can also let him/her know that you will not participate in any conversations or interactions that are not respectful or productive. You can confirm that you will treat your spouse with respect. It may be helpful to think of your relationship as a business partnership. Business partners usually negotiate in a civil and respectful manner. Focus on how you want things to be when you divorce and think and act in a way that will help you get to that future.

If you have tried all of the above and still have a few issues that you simply cannot agree about, work with a certified, professional family mediator on those specific issues. Focusing on a narrower set of issues will limit the amounts of time and money you spend on a mediator.

CHAPTER 3

Taking Care of Yourself as Your Life Changes

Even if you initiated the separation, you may experience all of the emotions of grieving over the loss of your partner or the loss of the life you had. You may feel terrified about what is going to happen next and when the nightmare will end. You may feel depressed about the burdens you now carry and the financial limitations of your current situation. You need to take care of yourself.

A support group can be wonderfully helpful. Using the Internet, you may find a Meetup group, a group in a community service center, or a faith-based divorce recovery group that suits you.

This is a good time to ask friends just to listen. Simply having someone who listens and cares can help a lot. You may want to ask your friends not to give you too much advice, because friends and relatives often give contradictory and ill-informed advice. The fact that your cousin got spousal support for ten years does not mean that you should expect the same outcome or have it as your goal. If you need to talk often about how you are feeling and how you are doing, it may be a good idea to talk with several friends. Leaning too much on one individual for emotional support can exhaust and destroy a friendship.

You may need to ask some of your relatives and friends not to be overly sympathetic. Getting stuck in a victim mentality, endlessly blaming your ex for ruining your life, is not good for your heart or your soul. The best friends and counselors can care about you and also help you be honest with yourself about your role in contributing to the need for a divorce. They can also help you notice when you are forgetting to embrace opportunities to make positive changes in your life and in your attitude.

If you are dealing with intense hostility, anxiety, and/or depression, professional counseling may help you get through this difficult time. Keep in mind that counselors and therapists are like doctors and plumbers: Some are very good at what they do; some have questionable levels of competence; some actually do more harm than good. Also, it is important to find a good fit. A counselor who did a great job for one of your friends may not click with you. Interviewing more than two therapists may serve you well.

Your faith community, if you have one, can be a great resource. Some churches, temples, and mosques have trained people who provide counseling. Others may be able to direct you to people in the community who can help you during hard times. A community family center or mental health center may have good counselors available at low cost. Some organizations labelled as

Women's Centers actually provide affordable services for men and children as well as women.

For your children's sake as well as your own, you need to take care of yourself. When an emergency occurs in an airplane, you are advised to put on your own oxygen mask before helping your child put on his or hers. The same advice applies during divorce. It is extremely difficult to give good care to your children if you are not taking care of yourself.

CHAPTER 4

Helping Your Kids Manage This Difficult Transition

Even when everything goes as well as it can, divorce requires everyone in the family to adjust to some big changes.

Most kids hate watching their parents fight and hate the fallout from parental battles. Protecting your children from those stresses should be a high priority for you and your spouse or ex. Many of the comments in this chapter relate to protecting your children from your arguments with your spouse.

Few things in life feel worse than giving up being with your kids full time. Going from having them all the time to half of the time or less can be extremely difficult, particularly for the parent who has done most of the child rearing. Try to focus on what is best for the kids, including what they will remember about this time in their lives when they look back. Will they remember a lot of arguing, fighting, and emotional drama? Or will they remember a smooth transition during which they felt loved by both of their parents? We hope that you and your spouse will both be able to cooperate to make life as good as it can be for your kids. Children should not have to be preoccupied with their parents' outbursts or struggles. They should be free to play and grow.

If you and your spouse can agree about how you want to raise your kids, that will make life easier for them. You may be able to discuss many of the relevant topics and make shared decisions without involving a professional.

Parenting Schedules

If possible, develop a schedule for when your children will spend time with each parent. Predictability – knowing when they will see mom or dad again – helps children feel more secure. Sometimes parents' work schedules and children's activity schedules drive decisions about when the kids will be with one parent and when they will be with the other. Sometimes parents have a good amount of freedom about designing their family schedules. Some decide that their children will do best if they spend about 50% of their time with each parent. Some decide that the children should live primarily with one parent and have well-planned opportunities to spend time with the other parent.

When you and your spouse have created a parenting schedule together and agreed to adhere to it, there is much less ambiguity and uncertainty for all involved. This often leads to a big reduction in arguments.

We will have much more to say about Parenting Plans in Chapter 6. This section of the book is about handling the early period near the time of your separation. Chapter 6 has the details for a long-term plan.

Children's Expenses

Sometimes the issues that lead to fights are related to expenses. If you are able to resolve some financial questions early, your kids are likely to benefit. As you think about a preliminary agreement about child support, consider things like haircuts, new shoes, sports, other extra-curricular activities, birthday parties, school supplies, and field trips. Which of those expenses will be included in routine child support? How will the other expenses be shared or divided? If the two of you can decide such matters now and put your agreements in writing, you will have fewer fights about details and logistics.

The Commonwealth of Virginia provides and uses guidelines for calculating recommended amounts of child support. We will say more about that in Chapter 8. This section is about short-term arrangements as you begin restructuring your family. You will probably want much more detail in your long-term Agreement.

Household Rules

What kind of rules do you think are important for your kids to adhere to? Can you and your spouse agree about bedtime, nutrition, video gaming, TV, Internet use, chores, allowances, homework, exercise, religion, and other matters? For example, is an M-rated video game or an R-rated movie OK for your kids? It is great if you can agree about most of these topics. If you don't agree, that does not have to be a big problem. Make sure that your child knows what rules apply in both of their homes, what other rules apply in one parent's house, and what additional or different rules apply in the other parent's house. Having clear rules will help your kids avoid conflict and confusion. If each of you can be consistent about the rules in your home, that will help your kids.

It can be challenging to be the parent with the stricter rules. You may think that the kids would rather be with their other parent because of the liberties they get with that parent. This is not a good reason to be "loose" with your rules. Keep the rules that you believe are important for your kids. They will probably respect you for doing so. Giving freedoms, privileges, and gifts is not what makes kids feel loved. Children feel loved when you spend quality time with them. Explain to them why you have your rules. Tell them that the rules exist for their benefit.

Make sure that your kids know what the consequences of disobeying rules will be. The kids may protest that it is not fair for you to take their iPod away for a week because they stayed out past curfew if you have not told them about that consequence in advance. Obviously you cannot anticipate every possible kind of bad behavior and announce a corresponding consequence. What you can do is tell your kids what the rules are and what types of consequences may follow if they disobey rules. Then follow through. If you do not, the kids will not take you seriously. Threatening consequences and then ignoring bad behavior generally produces bad outcomes. Inconsistency about enforcing rules can encourage laziness, defiance, and/or a lack of self-discipline in your child.

New Significant Others

In most cases, it is a good idea for divorcing parents to discuss rules about introducing new boyfriends or girlfriends into their children's lives.

No matter how great a new relationship might seem in the beginning, the reality is that a lot can change in the first few months. You and the person you are dating are just getting to know each other. What you do not know about each other is greater than what you do know. It may not be a good idea to expose your kids to a parade of potential stepparents.

Many family therapists recommend six months as a good time frame. If you have been dating for six months and you think the relationship may be serious and long-lasting, then maybe it is time for your kids and your dating partner to begin to get acquainted. Ideally, you and your spouse can agree on a time period that seems right for both of you and for your kids.

Your agreement with your ex-to-be can also say that neither of you will let a sexual partner stay overnight or even stay late into the evening when any of your kids are in the home.

Co-Parenting Counseling

If you and your ex have difficulty agreeing about schedules and rules, or if you fight with each other a lot, you may benefit from co-parenting counseling. In this form of counseling, you and your ex meet with a counselor to discuss parenting and communication issues. Most competent family therapists can provide this service. Co-parenting counseling provides a safe place to talk about the "hot topics" that are not easy for you and your ex to discuss on your own.

Consider preparing an agenda for each session and sharing it before your scheduled appointment. That way both of you will know what to be prepared to discuss. An agenda can help you focus and talk through as many specific issues as possible. This helps you get the most from the time and money you invest in counseling.

Finding Free or Low-Cost Counseling for Your Kids

If your child is able to talk directly with you about all of his or her feelings, that is great. Most kids are not comfortable doing so. If you can listen in an open, non-judgmental, and non-defensive way, encourage each of your children to talk to you. If you can honestly assure them that their questions and comments will be accepted and considered seriously, they may want to confide in you and may benefit greatly from the opportunity to do so. Many children, however, need to be able to confide in someone outside of their family.

If you have a school-aged child, free counseling for your child may be available at school. You can call your child's school and ask whether a school counselor is available. For Rebecca's family, this worked well. One son's school had a counselor who was someone he could talk to, away from each of his parents, to discuss his feelings about their divorce. If free counseling is available through your child's school, it may be a good resource for your child. Do pay attention though. If the counselor is available for only 20 minutes at a time and only right before the school day starts, he or she is not likely to be able to help your child much. Trying to talk to a distracted school counselor when the child could be enjoying time with friends may even make things worse.

If your child's school does not have a counselor for your child, a local county agency may have one. People in your faith community may also be able to recommend good counselors for your kids.

A government or nonprofit organization in your county may offer a program that provides free group therapy for your child. Do your homework before enrolling your child in one of these programs. Some are excellent. Others may expose your child to frightening stories and to children who have severe emotional problems. You may want to shelter your kids from stories of physical abuse, mental abuse, destructive behavior, and threats and weapons. Some distressed tweens and teens show rebellious behavior such as smoking, drinking, drug use, or shoplifting. You may not want to introduce your child to kids who are acting out in such ways. ("Acting out" is showing aggressive, destructive, or disruptive behavior. The child is acting out painful feelings instead of talking about them.)

There are some times when it is best to pay for the services you need. If good quality free counseling is not available, you may want to consider private therapy for your children. You can begin by checking your health insurance plan to see what it covers.

Therapy for Very Young Children

What if your children are very young? What kind of therapy options exist for preschool children? Why would a two-year-old need therapy when he or she talks mostly in two-word sentences? If you notice behavioral changes in your child that lead you to believe your child is distressed, your child may benefit from therapy.

Therapy for very young children is almost always play therapy. Rebecca's three-year-old son loved going to his therapist, playing with the toys and games she had, and playing in the sand. Kids this age express themselves mainly through play. Consequently play therapy can be an effective way to help them express themselves when they are too young to articulate their feelings.

Rebecca and her ex did not put their son in therapy right away when they separated. When his behavior showed that he was angry and upset and did not know how to manage his feelings, they found a good therapist for him. The therapist worked out a payment plan and billed each parent for half of the cost of the therapy sessions. Their son went to therapy every week for about four months. The therapist gave the parents some good feedback and insight about their son and some helpful suggestions for working with him outside of therapy. Although therapy was not free, insurance covered part of the cost. The remaining out-of-pocket expense was money well spent.

How You Treat Your Ex

The way you treat your ex impacts your kids and reflects on you. Regardless of how your relationship is now, you had one or more kids together. As long as your children and you are alive, you will probably have to share them. This is reality except in the rare cases when a court determines that one of you is unfit to be a parent and in the very sad cases in which one parent abandons the children or alienates them from the other parent. One good predictor of children's well-being after divorce is how well the parents are able to respect each other as parents and cooperate about parenting issues. Whether the parents like each other is not too important. How well they cooperate as parents affects the children much more.

You are a primary role model for your kids. The most powerful thing you can do for your kids is to lead by example. Kids do not do what you tell them to do. They do what they see you doing. If you yell and cry and belittle your ex, your children may have a hard time learning to manage their anger and resentment. If exposure to your ex stirs up too much negative emotion in you, try arranging your schedule so that face-to-face interactions with your ex are infrequent. You and your kids may benefit from the reduced occasions for conflict. Some ex-couples agree to limit their kids' exposure to fights by communicating only through text messages or email.

Books that many divorced parents have found helpful include *Raising the Kid You Love with the Ex You Hate*, by Ed Farber; *The Co-Parenting Survival Guide*, by Elizabeth Thayer and Jeffrey Zimmerman; and *Mom's House, Dad's House* and *The Co-Parenting Toolkit*, both by Isolina Ricci.

If you are having serious trouble communicating, do some research about resources for separated and divorced parents. For example, UpToParents.org and OurFamilyWizard.com have some great information and tools for mothers and fathers.

For parents who fight a lot, NewWaysForFamilies.com and HighConflictInstitute.com may be very helpful. You may also find other good sites or apps that work well in your particular situation.

If you and your ex cannot be friendly toward each other, spare your kids by keeping your interactions brief and businesslike. Take the high road. If you do not have anything nice to say, do not say anything at all. We know this is more easily said than done, but most people can recognize its importance.

Books for Children of Divorce

You can borrow and/or buy some children's books about separation and divorce. Rebecca read such books with her kids, and they talked about the books afterwards. Learning about others going through similar experiences helped the kids. Reading the books together with their mom created safe opportunities to discuss their feelings.

One of the books Rebecca liked was *Mama and Daddy Bear's Divorce* by Cornelia Maude Spelman. Another popular book is *Nina has Two Houses* by Danielle Jacobs. Both of those books are for young children. If you search for either of those titles in a library or in an online book store, you will also find many other books written to help kids handle the changes that come with divorce. There are many good books for children of various ages.

For all of us who are looking to budget wisely, the local library is a great resource. Your tax dollars are paying for libraries, so take full advantage. Librarians are trained to help you find books. They are likely to be knowledgeable about which books would be best for your kid's particular age and situation. Just ask.

If you spot a great book on the Internet but it is not in your local library's collection, the librarian may be able to get it from another branch or another library. On the other hand, purchasing an inexpensive book may be smarter than spending your time chasing it down in a library. If it is a book you or your kids will want to read over and over, it is worth buying.

Discussions and Interactions with Your Kids

Kids do not need to know and should not know all of the gruesome details of why you are getting divorced (e.g. mommy had an affair, or daddy gained sixty pounds and lost interest in sex). If you feel betrayed and abandoned or if your spouse is emotionally abusive to you, work with a therapist to handle those issues; do not vent your feelings about them in front of your kids. Do, however, help your children learn the life skills they need so that they will not fall into or tolerate abusive relationships.

Unless you have a reason to think that one parent is going to do a disappearing act, let your kids know that you are divorcing because you have changed and do not belong together anymore and assure them that Mom will always be their mom and Dad will always be their dad, and <u>both of you will always love them</u>. Also assure them that the divorce is not their fault. They did not cause it and they cannot fix it.

Kids often fear the unknown when it comes to changes in family circumstances. Keep an open dialogue with your kids. Acknowledge your children's feelings and reassure them that their feelings are normal. You can also reassure them that you are there to support them, listen, and help. Steer clear of blithely telling them that "everything is going to be fine." It is important for them to have their feelings acknowledged – whatever their feelings are. Divorce can be a tough transition, and their feelings about it may be very different from yours.

Bedtime, bath time, and playtime may provide great opportunities to have conversations with your kids. It is during these times that they are most likely to be relaxed, open, and talkative. With older children, times when just one is riding in the car with you can be good opportunities for your child to talk about things that matter to him or her.

Although it may be tempting to buy extra things for your kids to try to buy their love or to give them gifts out of guilt, this is not what makes children feel loved. Kids feel most loved when you give them attention and spend quality time with them. Do what is in their best interests, with a long-term vision in mind, not only what provides short-term gratification for the kids or for you.

CHAPTER 5

Getting Free or Low-Cost Legal Advice

The terms of your divorce will have far-reaching and long-lasting effects. We strongly recommend getting some legal advice about these decisions. You can do that without spending a large sum of money.

One of Rebecca's attorney friends recommended a website called Avvo™, www.avvo.com. It provides access to a community of lawyers (as well as doctors and dentists) to whom you can submit questions about your specific situation. Real lawyers provided free, timely answers to Rebecca's questions. The website also has a database of topics and questions that you can search. You may find the answer to your question right away. If not, the wait time to get a personalized answer was typically quite short. Rebecca's friend frequently answered questions there (receiving no compensation) because answering questions gave him exposure to potential new clients and helped him stay current in his knowledge of laws and court rulings. Often when you submit a question, you get answers from several attorneys. It is great to be able to compare answers from more than one attorney, and it's free.

There are several other websites that may be useful. They include www.justanswer.com and www.lawqa.com. They seem similar to Avvo™ and may be worth a look. We have no direct experience with these, but they are free and may be helpful. That said, we obviously cannot guarantee the accuracy of Avvo™ or any similar websites.

Another way to get free legal advice is to contact attorneys. Some provide respectable amounts of free information on their websites. Many offer a free or low-cost initial consultation. Of course they are hoping that after you talk with them you will want to hire them. Often you can get many questions answered during brief, free consultations with one or two attorneys. For Rebecca, this was a valuable option. In most areas, the local Bar Association will refer you to a short, low-cost consultation with an attorney.

We do not recommend calling a large number of attorneys to get free legal advice. It does not seem fair to waste their time answering your questions if there is no chance that you will hire them. More importantly, if you need that much help, you may need to retain an attorney, either because of the complexity of your case or because of your specific needs for assistance.

Your local county court may have a legal self-help center and may be able to tell you about free resources in your city or county. The court staff may know of lawyers who offer free advice at the family court on certain days or know of a free legal aid program. You should also check your county's Circuit Court website to see what information is readily available there. The court's website may include information about free legal resources and/or referral to a free or low-cost consultation with an attorney. Many courthouses also have law libraries with helpful librarians.

If you can read legalese, you can look up Virginia's domestic relations laws at http://leg1.state.va.us/cgi-bin/legp504.exe?000+cod+TOC2000000. You can also go to a public or university law library and look up case law precedents relevant to your dilemmas.

CHAPTER 6

Your Parenting Plan

Before you divorce, you and your ex will need to put your plan for your parenting schedule into writing. If one parent is abusive, addicted, mentally unstable, or otherwise unfit, you may need professional help deciding what to do. What will be best for your kids? When, where, and how (e.g., in the presence of other relatives, for safety's sake) should they spend time with that parent? If both parents are capable of keeping a child safe and reasonably healthy, then your job is to figure out what schedule will be best for your kids.

Based on solid scientific research, there is widespread agreement that children do best if they are able to maintain loving bonds with both parents and enjoy significant amounts of time with each parent. That said, there is wide variety in the schedules that suit different families.

Some families decide that the kids will spend one week with mom and the next week with dad, all through the year. For some kids, this works well. Obviously the parents' residences need to be fairly close to each other for this to work. For other kids, having just one home base during the school year works better.

Other families decide that every other weekend, short mid-week visits, and additional time during school breaks and summers add up to enough time with the non-residential parent. Some families designate one parent as the primary, residential parent during the school year and the other as the primary residential parent during the summer, while alternating weekends all year. There have even been families that decided the kids would live with the mom during the school year for two years and then live with the dad during the school year for two years while the kids were in elementary school. By the time they are in high school, most kids want to keep their full-time home base in the neighborhood where most of their friends live.

Many parents decide to take turns having the kids with them for Thanksgiving and other major holidays. Although this is a common plan, it may not be best for your kids. If, for example, the kids always spend Thanksgiving weekend with the father's extended family, always spend Christmas Eve with the father, and always spend Christmas day with the mother and her extended family, they can develop strong holiday traditions to treasure forever. In her book *The Pro Child Way: Parenting with an Ex*, Ellen Kellner advocates that sort of arrangement. While we do not agree with all of Ellen's advice, her book has a lot of useful guidance for divorced parents who want their children to grow up feeling secure and well loved.

Some ex-couples and their children do well with very simple parenting plans. Others need to include numerous details about matters such as these:

- specific times and locations for transferring the children from one parent to the other

- who provides transportation for the kids

- who arranges child care if one of the kids is sick and cannot attend school

- what to do if a parent has work-related travel that disrupts his or her routine parenting time

- what process they will use for agreeing on temporary changes to the schedule

- scheduled times for telephone or Internet communication between the non-residential parent and the child

- prohibitions against intruding on the other parent's time with the child by phoning or sending text messages to the child

- other details that are important to the parents and/or the children.

A mediator can help you develop the kind of parenting plan that will work best for your kids – anywhere from very simple to very detailed.

CHAPTER 7

Spousal Support (Alimony)

Although alimony (called "spousal support" in Virginia) was not an issue for either of us, many people facing divorce have questions and concerns. We can give you some information.

Spousal support consists of payments by one spouse to the other spouse for a specified period of time and sometimes for a specific purpose. For instance, support designed to help a spouse pay bills or maintain the financial status quo while a divorce is pending is called "temporary spousal support" or "*pendente lite* spousal support." In contrast, long-term spousal support may be designed to help an ex-spouse maintain the standard of living that the couple enjoyed during their marriage or may be designed to give the ex-spouse time to complete school or training and become self-supporting.

Temporary Spousal Support

As stated above, temporary spousal support is ordinarily paid, in appropriate circumstances, from whenever it begins until the divorce is finalized. When there is a disparity in incomes, responsibilities for children, or other relevant factors, the spouse with the lower income can ask for temporary spousal support. For instance, if a wife with a high income moves out of the family home where her low-income husband and their children still reside, someone still has to pay the family's bills. The husband may need spousal support to help him do that.

If the high-income spouse does not voluntarily agree to pay temporary spousal support, the low-income spouse can petition the local Juvenile and Domestic Relations District Court to issue an order for temporary spousal support. For the period when a husband and wife are separated but not yet divorced, many courts in Virginia now use formulas developed in Fairfax County to determine the amount of spousal support. As this book goes to press, these are the formulas: If child support is not involved, then spousal support will ordinarily be 30% of the gross income of the spouse who earns more minus 50% of the gross income of the spouse who earns less. If child support is also involved, then spousal support will ordinarily be 28% of the gross income of the spouse who earns more, minus 58% of the gross income of the spouse who earns less.

For example, if the higher-wage spouse earns $80,000 per year, the lower-wage spouse earns $30,000 per year, and they have no minor children, the formula recommends $9,000 per year, which equals $750 per month. (30% of $80,000 = $24,000; 50% of $30,000 = $15,000; and $24,000 – $15,000 = $9,000.) If the parties do have minor children, then the formula recommends $5,000 per year, which equals $417 per month. (28% of $80,000 = $22,400; 58% of $30,000 = $17,400; and $22,400 – $17,400 = $5,000.) In addition to spousal support, the parent with the higher income is likely to pay child support. That is why the formulas reduce spousal support when there are minor children.

Although these guidelines for *pendente lite* spousal support are used in many of Virginia's courts, the law does not require them at the Circuit Court level.

The parties can choose to settle on a different amount of temporary spousal support for a variety of reasons. They can work this out on their own, arrange it by working with a professional family mediator, or ask their attorneys to negotiate an acceptable amount. When the decision is made, be sure to put it into a written Agreement signed by both spouses. If the matter is left to a judge to decide, the court may also deviate from the formula if the judge is persuaded that there is a good reason to do so, and many reasons can be considered.

When deciding about spousal support, temporary or long-term, consider the tax consequences. Spousal support is deductible for the spouse who pays it and is taxable income for the spouse who receives it *if* the support is paid pursuant to a written Agreement or a court order. In some cases spousal support transfers some income from a higher tax bracket to a lower tax bracket, thereby leaving more money somewhere in the family. That seems likely to be good for the kids.

Long-Term Spousal Support

When the divorce is finalized, the rules for spousal support change radically. The formulas described above become completely irrelevant. Many factors can influence what amount of spousal support is to be paid and for how long. Often the spouse with the higher income pays spousal support for about half as many years as the marriage lasted, but no formula or rule is used with any consistency.

While you are negotiating the terms of your divorce, with or without help from a mediator or an attorney, you may find the list of factors that judges consider useful. In words that are abbreviated and simplified here, Virginia's Code (§ 20-107.1) says that, to determine the nature, amount, and duration of spousal support, the court shall consider the following:

1. The obligations, needs, and financial resources of the parties, including income from pension, profit-sharing, or retirement plans;

2. The standard of living established during the marriage;

3. The duration of the marriage;

4. The age and physical and mental condition of the parties and any special circumstances of the family;

5. The extent to which the age, physical or mental condition or special circumstances of any child of the parties would make it appropriate that a party not seek employment;

6. The contributions, monetary and non-monetary, of each party to the well-being of the family;

7. The property interests of the parties, both real and personal, tangible and intangible;

8. The provisions made with regard to the marital property under § 20-107.3 (i.e., who gets which assets and debts);

9. The earning capacity, including the skills, education and training of the parties and the present employment opportunities for them;

10. The prospects, time, and costs involved for a party to acquire education, training, and employment to enhance his or her earning ability;

11. The decisions regarding employment, career, economics, education and parenting arrangements made by the parties during the marriage and their effect on present and future earning potential, including the length of time one or both of the parties have been absent from the job market;

12. The extent to which either party has contributed to the attainment of education, training, career position or profession of the other party; and

13. Such other factors, including the tax consequences to each party, as are necessary to consider the equities between the parties.

People often agree that long-term spousal support is appropriate when one spouse quit his or her job during the marriage to raise the couple's children. After eight or ten years at home, that person's job skills may need to be updated. Even if he or she can get a job right away, it will take some years of climbing up the income ladder before his or her income will be similar to the income of the parent whose career was uninterrupted.

You can agree in advance that spousal support may be reviewed or amended if either party's financial situation changes significantly. If your Agreement does not include a statement about modifying spousal support in the future, then it will not be possible for a court to modify it.

Another factor to consider when making spousal support decisions is what will happen when the person who is paying support retires. If a court decides the matter of spousal support, then the amount can be modified if there is a "material change in circumstances." One party retiring at a reasonable retirement age can create a material change that most courts would treat as relevant. If the amount of spousal support is decided by an

Agreement, then a court can modify it only to the extent that the Agreement permits. The parties can agree in advance about how they will modify spousal support when one or both reach retirement age or they can agree that they will re-evaluate and modify spousal support when one retires. If they say nothing about future modifications, then the amount stated in the Agreement cannot be modified by a court.

Decisions about spousal support are often linked to decisions about who gets which marital property and which marital debts. Often both decisions about spousal support and decisions about who gets what are included in one Separation and Property Settlement Agreement.

Amounts and durations of spousal support vary widely. Some people (usually men) who made substantially more money than their exes are paying spousal support indefinitely because their marriages lasted a long time and the way they defined their roles during the marriage made the ex-spouse economically dependent on the breadwinner. In contrast, because of changes in roles, some women are paying spousal support to their ex-husbands. The husband being the stay-at-home parent is more common than it once was. In other cases, receiving a significant amount of spousal support for just three to five years is enough to help the lower-income spouse update some skills, gain some experience, and be well-positioned to be self-supporting when that period ends.

In her family mediation practice, Virginia has seen a huge variety of decisions about what amount of spousal support would be appropriate and for how long. Spouses who are divorcing often discuss several of the thirteen factors listed near the start of this section as they make their decisions.

Deciding about long-term spousal support can be a complex endeavor. Spousal support is often a litigated issue. As previously noted, we recommend doing a sober cost-benefit analysis before starting a long court battle over spousal support or anything else. Sometimes the cost in attorney fees will be greater than any reduction or increase in support a party might win *if* the court rules in his or her favor. In most cases it is best if you and your ex can come to an agreement about what amount of spousal support is reasonable and for how long, given the specific details of your situation.

Because the total amount of spousal support over the course of years can be substantial, if you are in a situation where spousal support seems appropriate and you are having trouble coming to an agreement with your ex, we recommend that you seek advice from an attorney to protect your interests. You can also work with a family mediator to help you and your spouse discuss a variety of options and rationales and develop an agreement about spousal support.

As previously stated, the person who pays spousal support deducts it from his or her taxable income and the person who receives spousal support adds it to his or her taxable income if the support is paid as a result of a written Agreement or a court order. This sometimes transfers some income from a higher tax bracket to a lower tax bracket, which results in more money being available for the former spouses to divide or to put into a college fund or trust fund for their children.

Spousal support ends automatically when either party dies. It also ends automatically when the person receiving support remarries. In accordance with Virginia Code § 20-109A, spousal support ends automatically when the receiving spouse or ex lives with someone else in a relationship that closely resembles marriage for longer than twelve months.

CHAPTER 8

Child Support

A divorced dad once described what he thought about child support as follows: "My ex-wife committed the crime of taking my child away from me, and now I have to pay her for it." That is how it may feel to a non-residential parent who never wanted the spouse and child to stop living with him or her.

The law takes a different view: Even if your marriage did not work out, each parent has a duty to contribute to the child's financial support and general well-being. The residential parent contributes financially by paying his or her share for food, shelter, clothing, etc. Some people believe that if you can be employed without causing harm to your child, then you should have a job.

Financial support from the non-residential parent is also the child's right. That parent is helping to pay for what the child needs: food, shelter, clothing, day care, and health care. It may feel as if you are giving money to your ex, but the support is for your child. Without that financial support, your child's life would probably be much worse. If you are able to have a job, then you should be paying child support.

An appallingly high percentage of kids who live in single-parent families live in poverty. Living in or at the edge of poverty too often brings deprivation, suffering, and a lack of safety. We have known single parents who declined, for various reasons, to seek child support from the other parent. The results for the children often included having one over-worked, exhausted, frequently unavailable parent and one absentee parent. That is not a good situation for a child. Even when poverty is not an issue, child support matters. It can make the difference between being just barely okay financially and being comfortable financially. Which way do you want your child to grow up?

Some single parents appear to be doing fine supporting their kids financially and psychologically without help from the other parent. They do fine on their own – until it is time for college. Then the absence of the financial support the non-residential parent could have been paying for the past fifteen years becomes visible, because the residential parent has not been able to save money to help the child go to college. Earning a college degree makes a big difference in a person's earning power for the rest of his or her life. Finishing college without huge debts for student loans puts a young adult way ahead of the peers who will be repaying their loans for the next twenty or thirty years.

Bottom line: be a good parent. Love your child more than you hate your ex, and prove it by sending financial support for your child. If you think you cannot count on your child's other parent to use the money wisely to support your child, then maybe you can negotiate an arrangement for you to pay for specific things that you think are worthwhile and for the other parent to acknowledge acceptance of those payments as child support. You can also start a college savings account for your child that does not involve your ex.

The Commonwealth of Virginia has guidelines for calculating what amount of child support is likely to be appropriate in various situations. Factors you need for the worksheet calculations include:

- the number of children

- the number of days per year they spend with each parent

- the gross income of each parent

- how much spousal support is changing hands

- how much each of you pays for work-related child care expenses, and

- how much each of you pays for health insurance for the children.

A little online searching may help you find other factors that are relevant in your specific situation, such as the tax consequences of being self-employed or a duty to pay support for minor children from a prior relationship. For child support calculations, a child is a minor until he or she is 18 years old and has graduated from high school or until the child is 19 years old, whichever comes first.

If you leave the decision to a court, the presumption will be that the amount of support the guidelines recommend is appropriate. Virginia's Code does list a number of reasons why deviating from the guideline amount might be reasonable. In discussions with your ex, in mediation, or in a settlement conference with your lawyers present, you have even greater flexibility in deciding how much child support makes sense and can be paid in your family's circumstances.

There are online child support calculators, but be careful. Some are not up-to-date. The legislature changed the guidelines effective July 1, 2014. Also you may not know enough about whether to use a sole custody worksheet, a shared custody worksheet, or a split custody worksheet. A state-certified family mediator, a family law attorney, or someone at the nearest state office of Child Support Enforcement can do the worksheet calculations for you.

Parents can agree to an amount of child support that differs from the guideline recommendation for a variety of reasons. The residential parent may want the other parent to be able to use some of his or her time and money for higher education so that a year or two later that parent can contribute significantly more financial support for the children. In that case, the residential parent might agree to accept a lower amount of child support temporarily. A non-residential parent may agree to pay more than the guidelines require so that the child can attend a private school and take tennis or music lessons, not just have food, shelter, clothing, after-school care, and health care.

Many parents consider college to be almost a necessity for their children. For that reason, it is a good idea for you to include it in your child support agreement. Unless you include funding for post-high-school education in your Agreement, a court in Virginia cannot order a parent to pay child support during the child's college years.

A complete agreement about child support is likely to answer all of the following questions:

- How much child support will the nonresidential parent contribute each month?

- When did or when will the support obligation begin?

- How and when will payments be made?

- Is there an arrearage (an amount that should have been paid before the date of your Agreement but has not yet been paid)? If so how much is it? When and how will it be paid?

- Who will be responsible for providing health insurance for the children?

- How will you share costs of children's unreimbursed health expenses, such as co-payments and portions of fees not covered by insurance? For example, if your child needs braces, surgery, or psychiatric care, those expenses can be large. Unless you agree on a different plan, the law says that each parent will be responsible for the portion of the medical expenses that matches his or her percentage of their combined gross income. If either parent's income is likely to change much or often, you may want to include a clause about recalculating those percentages annually.

- If you agree to share unreimbursed medical expenses, when and how will one parent reimburse the other for his or her share of a health care expense?

- When or under what circumstances will you recalculate the basic amount of child support?

- How will you make decisions about sharing unexpected but worthwhile expenses for your child that arise in the future? How will you decide whether a non-essential expense is worthwhile?

- What will either or both parents contribute to their child's education or training beyond high school?

Child support responsibilities can be modified. If any of the factors in the worksheet formula change significantly, the amount of child support the guidelines recommend may also change. If you think a modification is appropriate, you can petition the court to modify its child support order. If you and your ex work with a mediator to update your child support agreement, it is best to ask the court to incorporate your new Agreement into a modification of the prior court order. If you fail to do so, the court will continue to enforce the existing order.

CHAPTER 9

Getting Divorced *Pro Se* – Do-It-Yourself Divorce

Here is a brief overview of the steps in the legal process. This chapter is written for ex-couples who can reach agreement on all matters and who then want to complete the divorce process at minimal cost. If you cannot reach agreement, then you are likely to spend a lot of time and money on litigation.

Here are the five steps to an inexpensive divorce in Virginia:

Step 1: Make the decisions you need to make about the terms of your divorce.

Step 2: Put your decisions into a well-written Agreement and sign it.

Step 3: Prepare forms to file for divorce *pro se* (representing yourself).

Step 4: Take the forms to the Court Clerk's Office and pay the filing fee.

Step 5: Follow instructions from the Court to complete your divorce.

It is really that simple to get an inexpensive divorce in Virginia. Now let's go through the steps with a little more detail.

Step 1: You and your ex-to-be make the decisions you need to make.

If you have minor children, this step will include making decisions about the parenting schedule and child support. For everyone, Step 1 includes making decisions about spousal support and about who gets which marital property and who gets which marital debts. As you work on Step 1, you may decide that you want input from other professionals. Some people want to confer with a financial advisor. Some want to ask a child therapist about what will be best for their children. Most people want to include an attorney (to give you legal advice) and a mediator (to help you when negotiations become difficult).

You can complete Step 1 before you separate if both of you want to do so. For many couples, making the decisions about your parenting schedules, support, and distribution of assets and debts is not quick or easy. We addressed many of the components of this step in earlier chapters. You can find additional information about many relevant topics at colinfamilymediationgroup.com.

Step 1 is by far the most time-consuming step.

Step 2: Put your decisions into one or more well-written Agreement(s) and sign three copies in front of a notary public.

You can work with one professional family mediator and/or with one or two family law attorneys to write your Agreement(s). Many mediators write Agreements in plain English, not in legalese. When you have everything decided and recorded in a signed Property Settlement Agreement, you will be able to file for divorce *pro se*. (*"Pro se"* means representing yourself). The reason to sign three copies is so that each spouse can keep a signed copy and another signed copy can be given to the court in Step 4.

You can complete Step 2 as well as Step 1 before you separate if both of you want to do so. You can decide all the terms of your divorce before you separate or at any time after you separate. You can sign an enforceable Parenting Plan, an enforceable Support Agreement, and an enforceable Property Settlement Agreement as soon as you and your spouse are ready. You can develop and sign two or three separate agreements (one for the parenting schedule, one for support, and one for dividing your assets and debts) or put everything into one Agreement. Note that each Agreement you sign is likely to be enforceable. That is why we remind you that it is a good idea to consult an attorney before you sign one.

You can get everything decided and signed and you can divide your assets and debts long before you are eligible to file for divorce.

Step 3: Prepare the forms the court requires.

Instructions for preparing the proper forms for divorce are available online. For example, for Fairfax County, http://www.fairfaxcounty.gov/courts/circuit/pdf/fba-h-53.pdf has the Pro Se Divorce Package. It is a huge file. After you skip down pages and pages, you come to sample versions of each of the forms you have to provide. Unfortunately, they are not designed for filling in blanks electronically. As this book goes to press, the online instructions do not even make copying and pasting easy.

In many jurisdictions you can go to the Clerk's office for the Circuit Court, Civil Division, and pick up a copy of the *pro se* divorce package. Court personnel are prohibited by law from giving you legal advice or assistance, but they can tell you which forms to prepare.

Often one spouse or one spouse's attorney prepares all the paperwork. Occasionally, in very amicable divorces, Virginia has seen people share that work. Some people decide that preparing the necessary forms is such a chore that they are willing to pay an attorney $3,000 to handle it for them. As this book goes to press, it is not hard to find an attorney who will prepare all of your court paperwork for $3,000, provided that you already have a signed Property Settlement Agreement. New online services (of unknown quality) become available from time to time. If you do not want to spend $3,000 for what is mostly a secretarial task and you do not find good online resources, a lawyer, a mediator, or a legal aid clinic may be able to help you find a less expensive way to get your forms prepared.

Here is a list of what you will need to bring to the Circuit Court, Civil Intake Division. Laws and court procedures change from time to time, so this list may be incomplete.

- Divorce Case Coversheet, which is available from the Civil Intake Division and is also online at http://www.courts.state.va.us/forms/circuit/cc141 6.pdf

- The Divorce Complaint, which asks the Court to incorporate the terms of your Property Settlement Agreement into an Order for Divorce. ("Divorce Complaint" is the title for your request for the Court to declare you to be divorced.)

- VS-4 State Statistical Form (available from the Civil Court Intake Division)

- Filing Fees

- Service Fee if your spouse is not willing to sign the Waiver of Service. ("Service" refers to official delivery of the Divorce Complaint and related documents to your spouse.)

- Acceptance/waiver of service form, which is available at http://www.courts.state.va.us/forms/circuit/cc140 6.pdf

- Addendum for Protected Identifying Information - Confidential - State Form CC-1426

- Order for Divorce

- Request for *Ore Tenus* Hearing Form ("*Ore Tenus*" means oral. At an *Ore Tenus* hearing, the judge listens to what you and a witness say.)

- A copy of your signed, notarized Property Settlement Agreement.

Instead of asking for an *Ore Tenus* hearing, you can present evidence of having lived separate and apart from each other for enough months by affidavit (a written statement confirmed by oath or affirmation). A cost-benefit analysis may be helpful. What will it cost, in time and money, to have a lawyer interview you and your witness and have a court reporter create the affidavit? What will it cost in time and parking fees for you and your witness to attend a short hearing? If you have been living separately under the same roof, some judges may not accept proof by affidavit; a court hearing may be necessary.

Step 4: Take the forms to the court and pay the modest filing fees.

You must wait for the minimum amount of time to pass after your date of separation before you file for divorce. If you have minor children, you cannot file for a no-fault divorce until you have lived apart from each other for at least twelve months. If you do not have minor children and do have a complete Settlement Agreement, you can file for divorce six months after your date of separation.

At the appropriate time, take all of the above forms and documents to a Circuit Court and find the Court Intake Office that handles Civil cases (not Criminal cases). The Clerk will tell you if there are any glaring errors or omissions. If the paperwork looks satisfactory, he or she will assign a case number.

The sum of the filing fees varies a bit from one jurisdiction to another and increases slightly if one of you plans to change your name as a result of the divorce, but the total is usually less than $105 (as this book goes to press). All fees are payable to the Clerk of the Circuit Court by cash, cashier's check, or money order. Personal checks and credit cards are not accepted.

Step 5: Follow instructions from the Circuit Court to complete your divorce.

Sometimes the Court Clerk finds a few things that you did not get quite right as you prepared your forms. The Clerk will let you know what needs to be corrected. When the forms are correct, the second party in the divorce signs the prepared Acceptance/Waiver of Service form. Then the court will put your case on the fast track for uncontested divorces and schedule a short *Ore Tenus* hearing.

At least one of you must attend this hearing and bring a witness (not your spouse) who can verify that you and your spouse have been living separately for the required number of months. Often the hearing lasts only ten minutes. Then you wait for the court to process the paperwork. Reasonably soon, your Divorce Order arrives in the mail.

This five-step system for getting an uncontested divorce is not the only way to get divorced in Virginia. It is simply the least expensive good road to divorce. You are free to talk with attorneys about the pros and cons of other approaches.

Conclusion

We have given you the basic steps and a general overview of the divorce process in Virginia, but we cannot, in this short book, cover everything you need to know. We encourage you to use free resources to educate yourself. We strongly recommend that you meet with a family law attorney at least once to get advice about the specifics of your situation.

As we said in the introduction, the divorce process may seem overwhelming, but getting started is not that difficult. How you approach this new chapter in your life is your choice. One phase of your life is ending, but another is beginning, and the new phase may turn out to be very fine indeed. It's your life; you can influence what happens next. The choices you make now can have a positive impact on the future you and your children will have. We hope this book will help you in your journey toward a new beginning and a secure, joyful life for yourself and your family.

Websites Mentioned

Avvo.com

ColinFamilyMediationGroup.com

HighConflictInstitute.com

NewWaysForFamilies.com

OurFamilyWizard.com

Searchable Mediator Directory of the Supreme Court of Virginia
(http://www.courts.state.va.us/courtadmin/aoc/djs/progra ms/drs/mediation/searchable_mediator_directory.html)

UpToParents.org

Virginia's Laws about Domestic Relations
(http://law.lis.virginia.gov/vacode)

About the Authors

Virginia L. Colin, Ph.D.

Formerly a research psychologist, Virginia Colin has been providing family mediation services since 1999. She is the Director of Colin Family Mediation Group and is a founding member of the Academy of Professional Family Mediators. Dr. Colin is the author of *Human Attachment*, "Divorce in Virginia," "Infant Attachment: What We Know Now," and other print and Internet publications. She is the host of the Internet talk radio program *Family Matters* on www.VoiceAmerica.com. She has been a foster parent, a married parent, a single parent, and a happily remarried stepparent. She and her husband together have five adult children. She enjoys Eurogames, theater, and gardening. Her website is colinfamilymediationgroup.com.

Rebecca A. Martin, CPA

A Certified Public Accountant, Rebecca Martin has been working in the financial services industry for over 15 years. She is a graduate of the University of California at Santa Barbara with a degree in Business Economics. After handling her own divorce, she wrote *How to Get Divorced for Free in California*. She is the mother of two active boys and enjoys hiking, biking, boating, and skiing.

****

We Welcome Your Feedback!

Please tell us what you found helpful, what was unclear, and what additional information you needed. If you found an error in the book or some information that was not up-to-date, please let us know about that, too. You may leave comments at http://colinfamilymediationgroup.com/the-guide-to-low-cost-divorce-in-virginia/. It is okay to use a pseudonym when leaving comments.

****

Made in the USA
Charleston, SC
30 September 2015